AF394395

POP HITS

All This Time

Words & Music by Wayne Hector, Steve Mac & Lorne Tennant

'All This Time' was sung by Pop Idol 2003 winner Michelle McManus. She spent three weeks at No.1 from Jan 11–31, 2004. Michelle was born in Glasgow on May 8, 1980 and before finding fame, Michelle was the regional events manager in Scotland for Marriott Hotels. Co-writer Wayne Hector also wrote 'Flying Without Wings', 'Hey Whatever' and has had over 35 No.1 hits world-wide.

Hints & Tips: Be careful with the right hand fingering in the first four bars, and try to hold the notes for their full value.

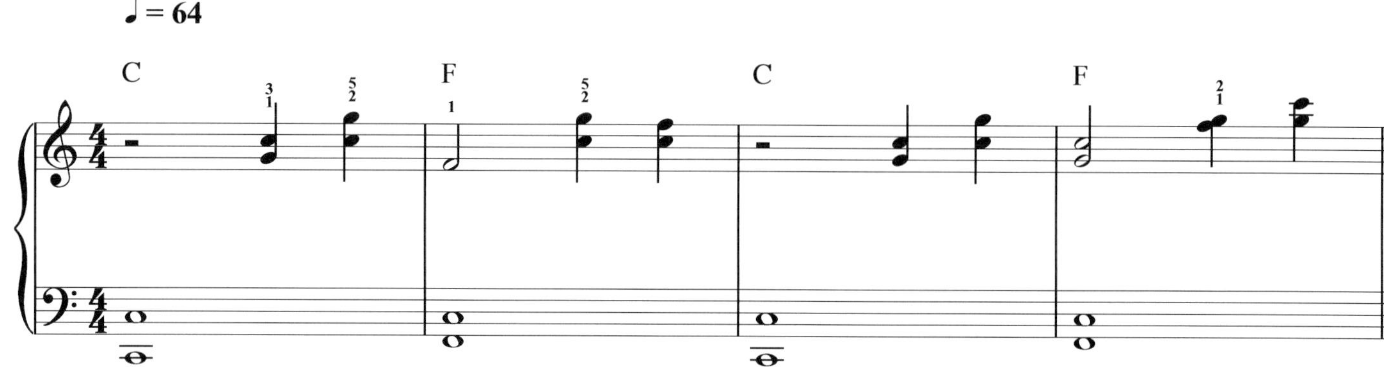

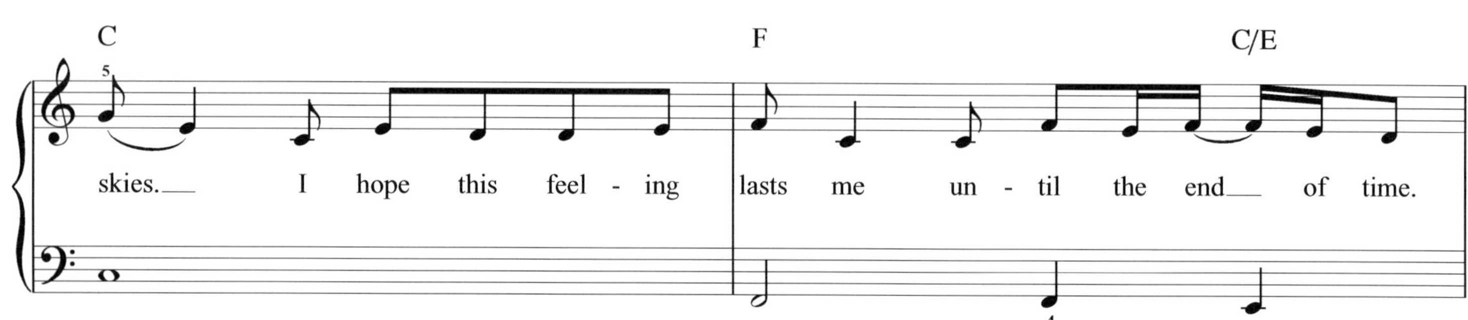

G
F
Now I don't see the things that bring me down like I used to, no.

G
F
C/G G7
C
Oh, there were times we felt like giv-ing up but we came through. All this time. We've come a

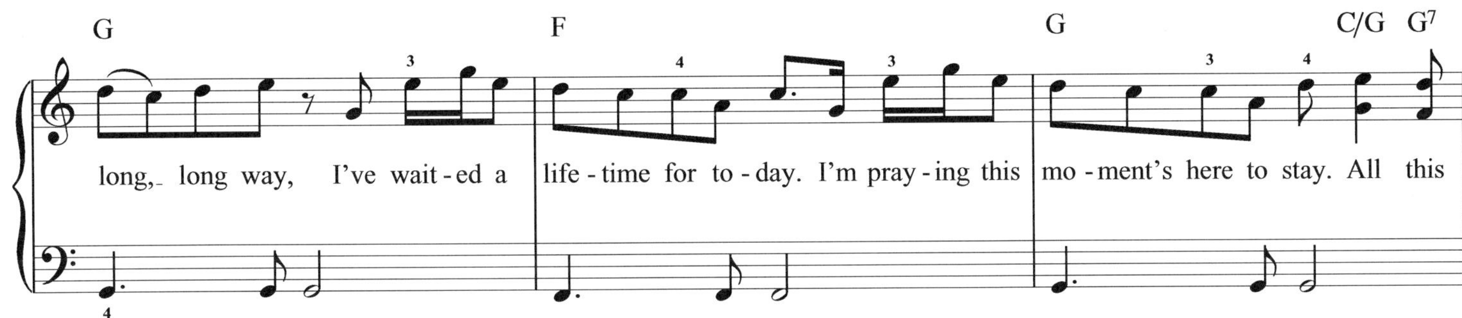

G
F
G
C/G G7
long, long way, I've wait-ed a life-time for to-day. I'm pray-ing this mo-ment's here to stay. All this

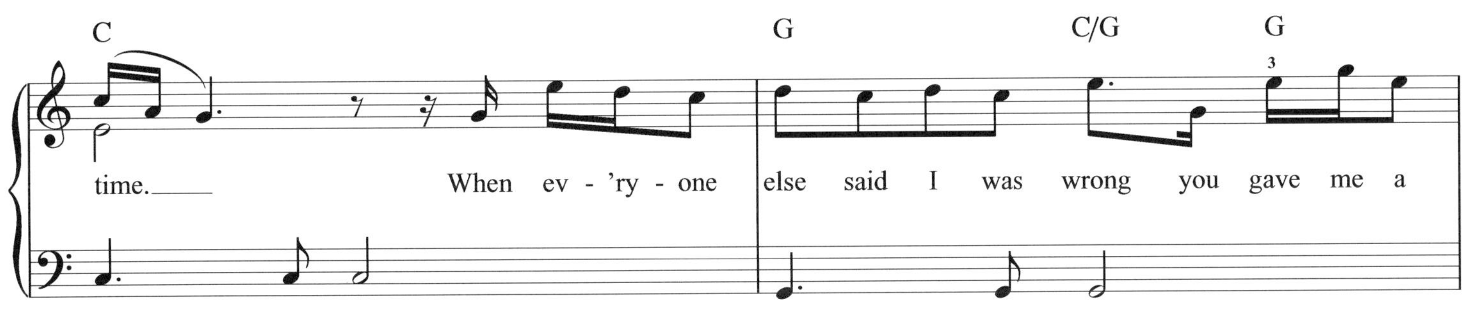

C
G
C/G
G
time. When ev-'ry-one else said I was wrong you gave me a

F
G
C/G G7
C
rea-son to be strong, you gave me the will to car-ry on. All this time.

Big Sur

Words By Conor Deasy
Music By Conor Deasy, Kevin Horan, Pádraic McMahon, Daniel Ryan & Ben Carrigan
Contains elements from "Theme From The Monkees" – Words & Music by Tommy Boyce & Bobby Hart.

'Big Sur' by The Thrills was released on May 26, 2003, and went into the UK chart at No.17.
The opening line provided the title for their No.3 début album, *So Much For The City*.
'Big Sur' also incorporates a line from 'The Theme From The Monkees' – see if you can spot where it is!
The Thrills band members are from Ireland and they all grew up together in Dublin.

Hints & Tips: Notice that this song should be played with a swing feel, with the second of
each pair of quavers (eighth notes) sounding shorter and softer than the first.

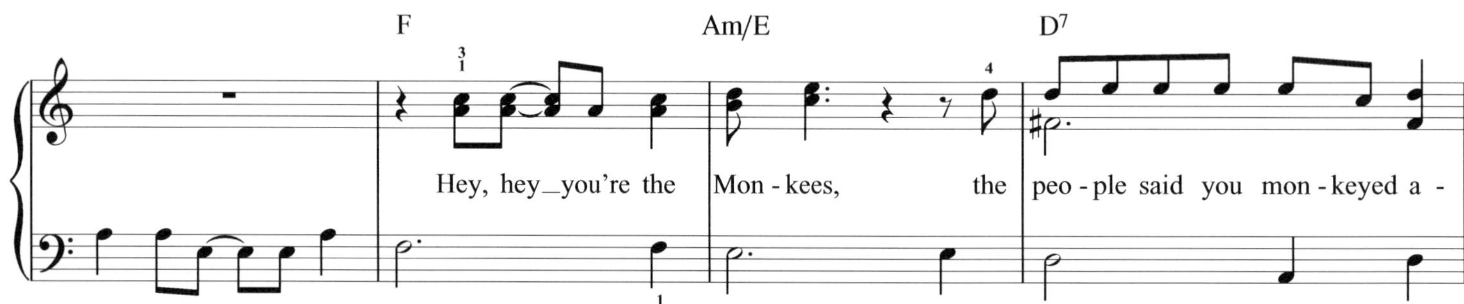

Am/E   F   N.C.   Am/E
- round,   but no - bo - dy's lis - ten - ing   now. (Do do do do do   do do.)

C   F   Dm   G
Just don't go back to Big Sur.

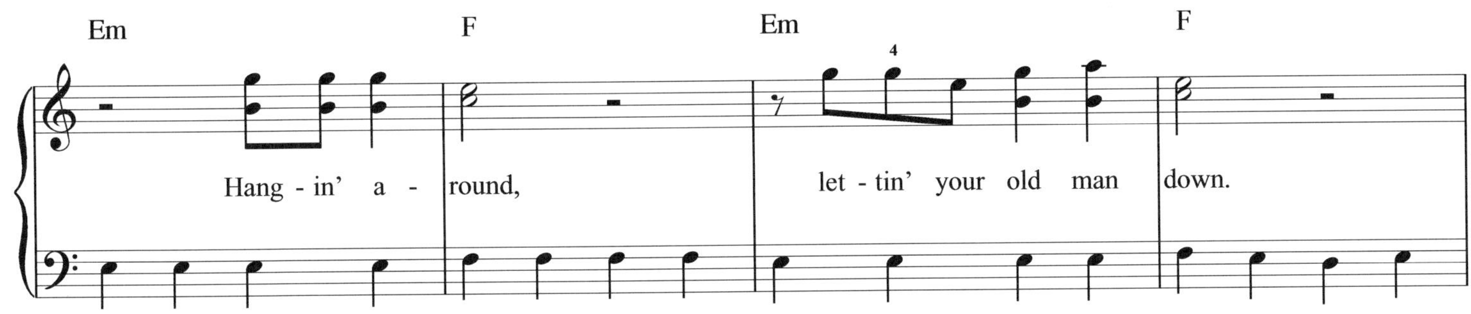

Em   F   Em   F
Hang - in' a - round,   let - tin' your old man down.

C   F   Dm7   G7
Just don't go back to Big Sur,   ba - by, ba - by please don't

F/C   G7   C
go.   Oh, ba - by, ba - by please don't go.

Changes

Words & Music by Ozzy Osbourne, Terence Butler, Terry Iommi & William Ward

'Changes' was originally recorded in 1972 by bat-eating rocker Ozzy Osbourne when he was in Black Sabbath.
The version in this book is the 2003 re-release in which Ozzy Osbourne collaborates with daughter Kelly.
Ozzy's career was revived recently when he and his family took part in the MTV show
The Osbournes in which cameras surveyed everyday life in the Osbourne family.

Hints & Tips: This is quite a slow song.
Keep a really steady tempo (speed) and don't be tempted to rush.

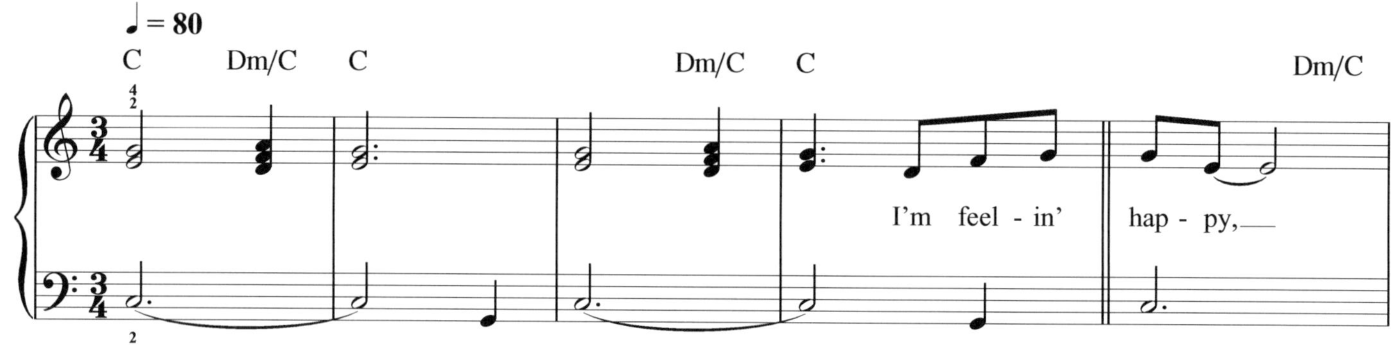

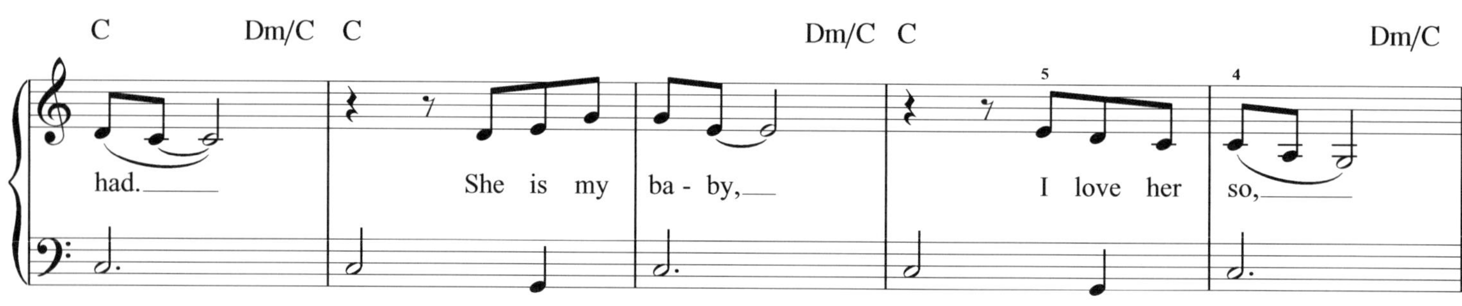

We're go - ing through chan - ges,
we're
go - ing through chan - ges.
We're go - ing through
chan - ges.
Chan -
- ges, chan - ges, chan - ges.
slowing

Clocks

Words & Music By Guy Berryman, Chris Martin, Jon Buckland & Will Champion

'Clocks' was recorded by super-band Coldplay, hitting the charts in April 2003 and remaining there for eight weeks. Coldplay are one of the most successful bands of the 21st century with two multi-platinum selling albums under their belt. The band met in the mid-'90s during their first week as students at University College London.

Hints & Tips: Practise the right hand alone for the first eight bars until the quavers (eighth notes) are absolutely even.

Em7   D   Am
oh, I beg, I beg and plead.__ Sing-ing: come out with things un-said.__
Em7   D   Am
Shoot an ap-ple off my head.__ And a trou-ble that can't be named.__ A
Em7
ti-ger's wait-ing to be tamed.__ Sing-ing: you
are,____ are.__
D
Am   Em

The Closest Thing To Crazy

Words & Music by Mike Batt

'The Closest Thing To Crazy' was recorded by elfin chanteuse Katie Melua and went to No.10 in the UK singles chart in December 2003. The album from which it came, *Call Off The Search*, reached No.1 in January 2004. Katie was born in Georgia in the former USSR in 1984 and moved to Belfast when she was nine. 'The Closest Thing To Crazy' was written by Mike Batt who also wrote 'The Wombling Song' and 'Bright Eyes'!

Hints & Tips: There are a lot of changes of time signature in this song. They should be no problem provided you feel a steady crotchet (quarter note) pulse throughout.

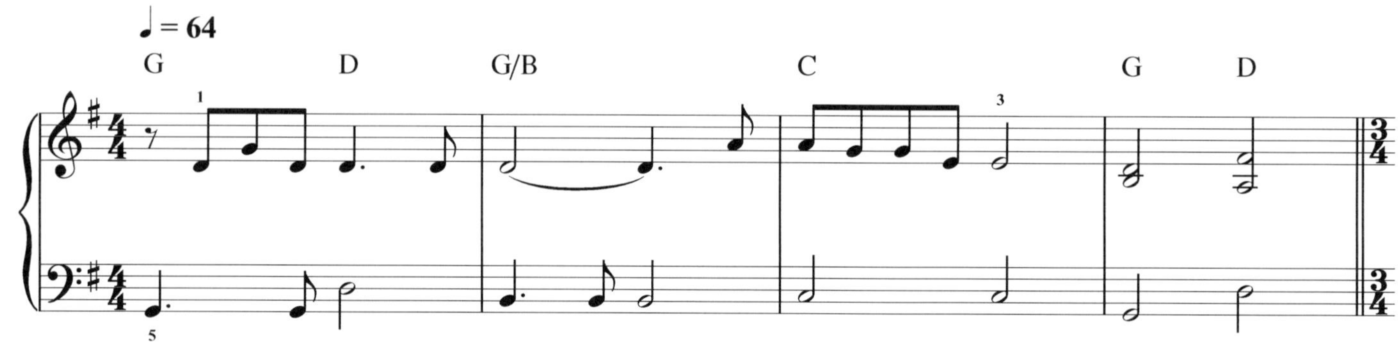

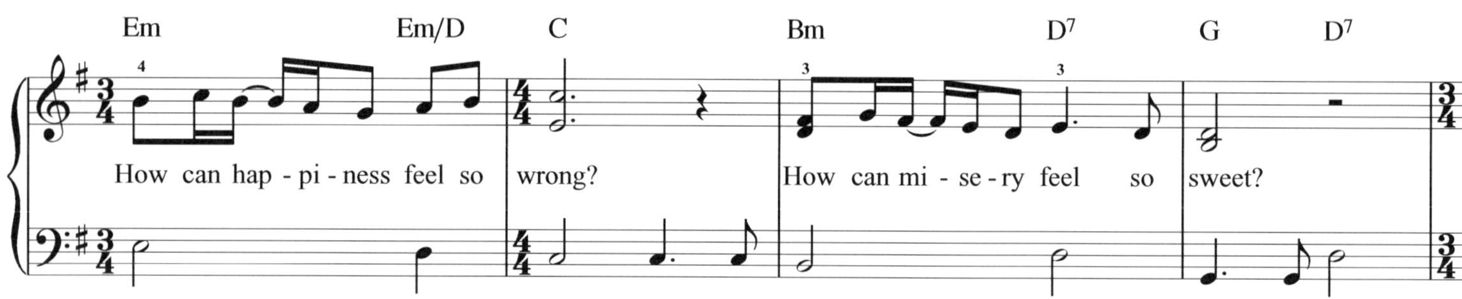

Em   Em/D   C   Bm   D   G   D7
How can I__ have got in so deep? Why did I__ fall in love with you? This is the

G   Em7   Am
clos - est thing to cra - zy I have ev - er been. Feel - ing twen - ty two, act - ing

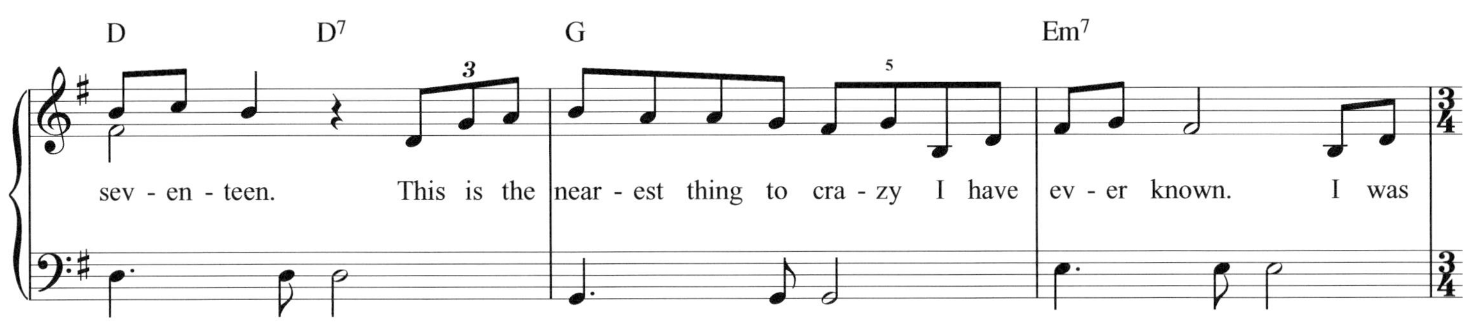

D   D7   G   Em7
sev - en - teen. This is the near - est thing to cra - zy I have ev - er known. I was

Am7   Cm   G   Em   C
nev - er cra - zy on my own and now I know__ that there's a link be - tween the

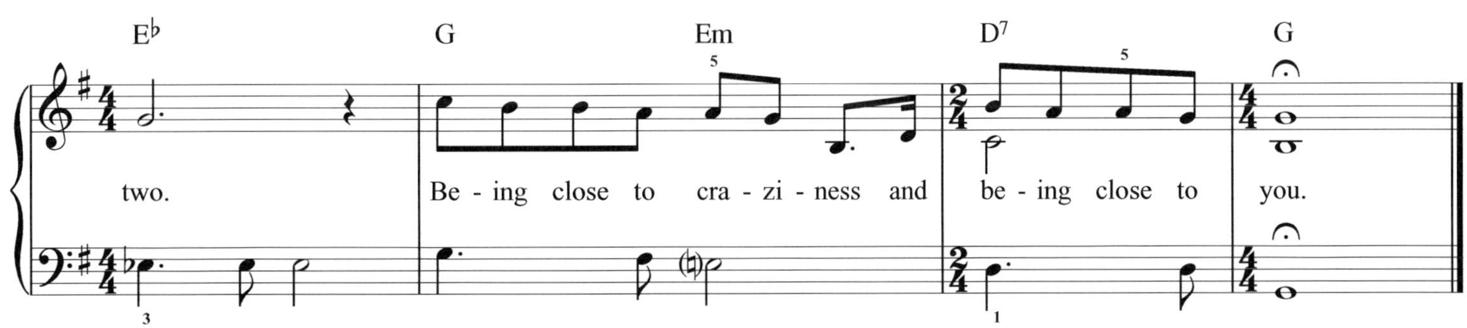

Eb   G   Em   D7   G
two. Be - ing close to cra - zi - ness and be - ing close to you.

Cry

Words & Music by Alex Parks, Gary Clark & Boo Hewerdine

'Cry' was recorded by Fame Academy 2003 winner Alex Parks. She comes from Mount Hawke,
a tiny village near Truro in Cornwall, and it was her Dad who actually entered her for the show.
Prior to Fame Academy, Alex was planning to move to Amsterdam to learn clowning!

Hints & Tips: When you are playing chords in the left hand make sure that both notes sound exactly together.
Try to feel the shape of the chord before you play it.

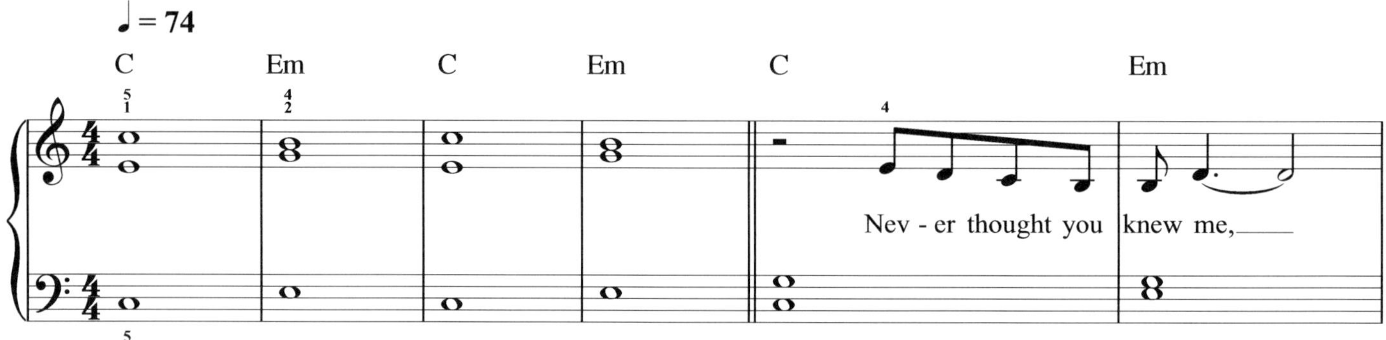

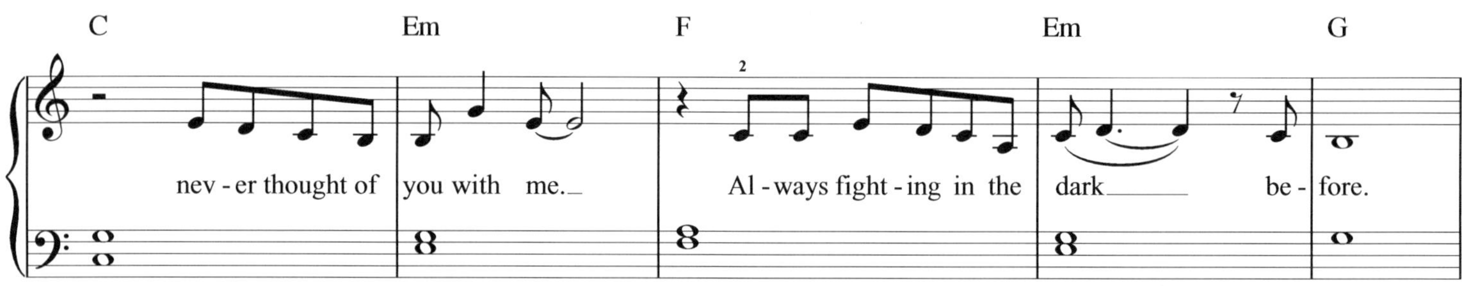

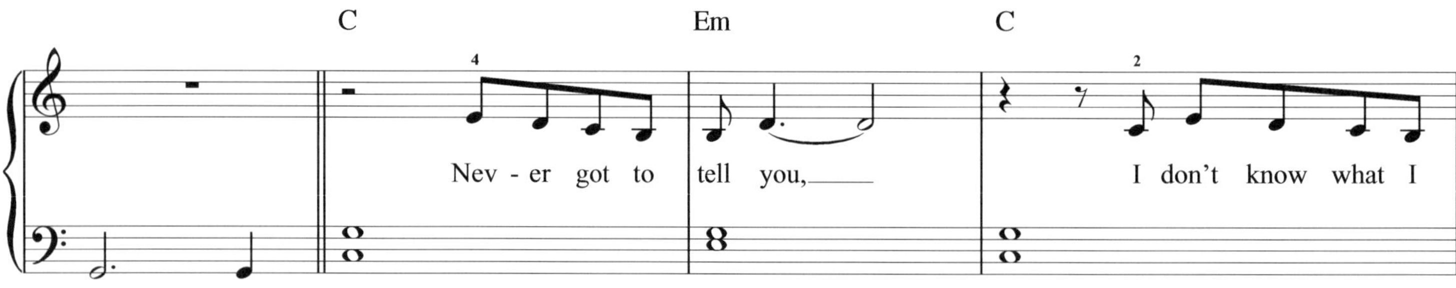

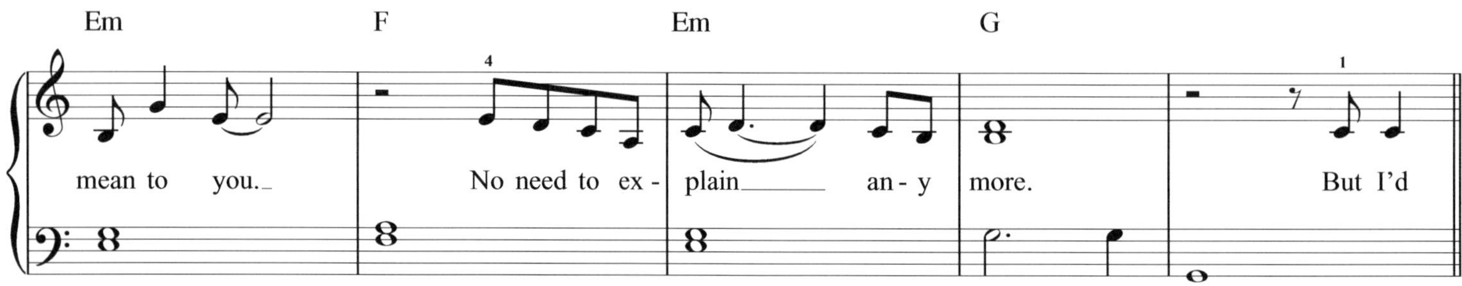

F G Am7 G F G
cry, ______ I would die if I lost you. Oh.__ And I'd cry, ______

Am7 G F G
______ Ooh. And you know you held me up, held me to the sun when I was

F G F
yours. And I know I let you down, let you down the day that I was gone.__

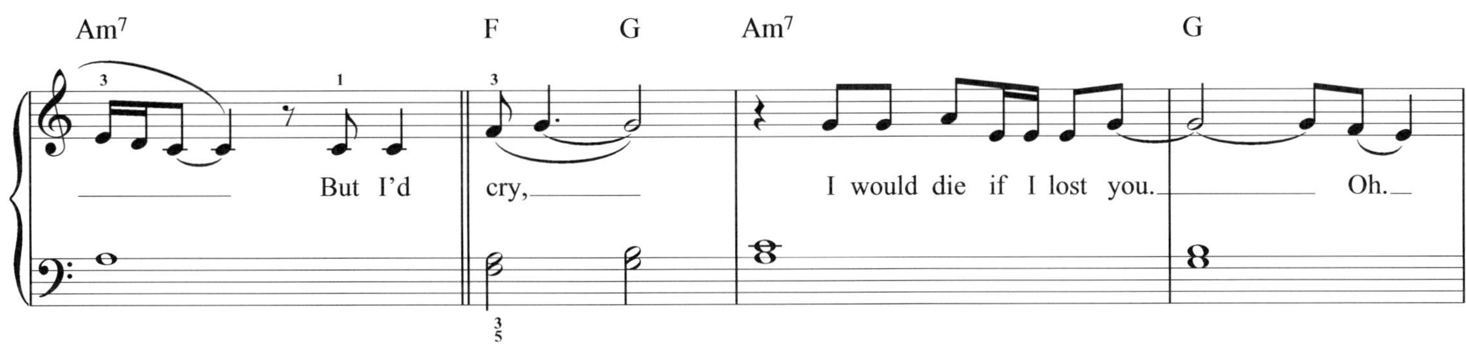

Am7 F G Am7 G
______ But I'd cry, ______ I would die if I lost you. ______ Oh.__

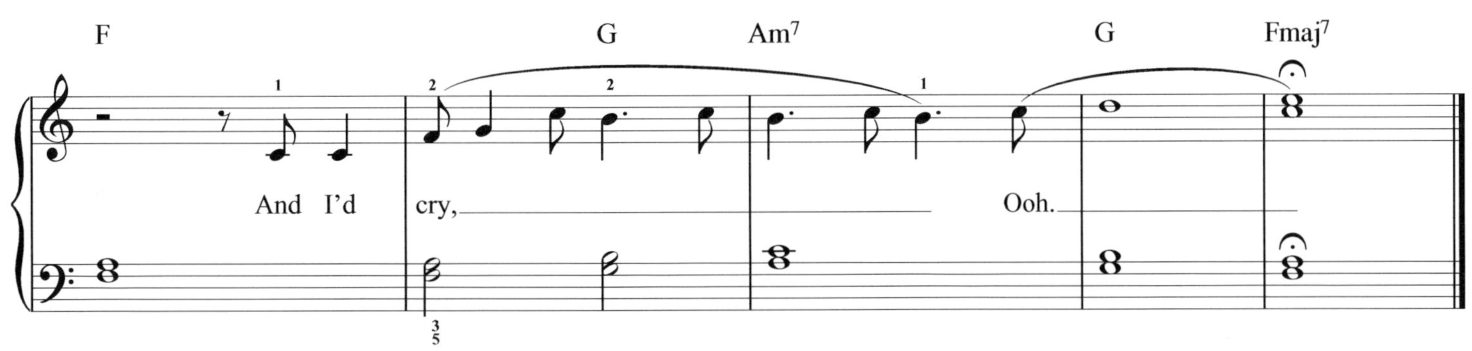

F G Am7 G Fmaj7
And I'd cry, ____________ Ooh. ______

Guilty

Words & Music by Duncan James, Gary Barlow, Tim Woodcock & Eliot Kennedy

'Guilty' was recorded by boy-band Blue in 2003. It went in at No.2, staying in the charts for nine weeks. Blue are made up of four London lads, Duncan James, Anthony Costa, Lee Ryan and Simon Webbe, and they released their first single in May 2001. Since then they've enjoyed much chart success and have won many prestigious awards.

Hints & Tips: To help you with the rhythm in the right hand, keep the left hand really steady.

C   G   C   F   C
mind?__   If it's wrong to do what's right I'm pre-pared to tes-ti-fy,__ if lov-in' you with all my heart's a

Am7   G   Am7   C
crime,   then I'm guilt-y.   Girl, I fol-low my heart,__   fol-low the truth,__

G   Em7   Am   Am7   C
__ right from the start.__ He led me to you, please don't leave me this way,__ I'm guilt-y, now all_

Dsus   D   G   C
__ I have to say... If it's wrong to tell the truth what am I sup-posed to do when

G   C   G
all I wan-na do is speak my mind?__ If it's wrong to do what's right I'm pre-

C   F   C   Am7   G
-pared to tes-ti-fy,__ if lov-in' you with all my heart's a crime,   then I'm guilt-y.

Heaven

Words & Music by Bryan Adams & Jim Vallance

'Heaven' was originally written and recorded by Brian Adams in 1985. The version here is based on the cover by DJ Sammy, released 2002. It reached No.1 remaining in the charts for an incredible 19 weeks. Born on the Spanish island of Mallorca in 1969, DJ Sammy began his music career as a DJ playing at clubs around the Balearics. He is now one of Spain's most successful producer DJs.

Hints & Tips: Practise the left hand chords until you really know them, and take care to make all the notes in each chord sound exactly together.

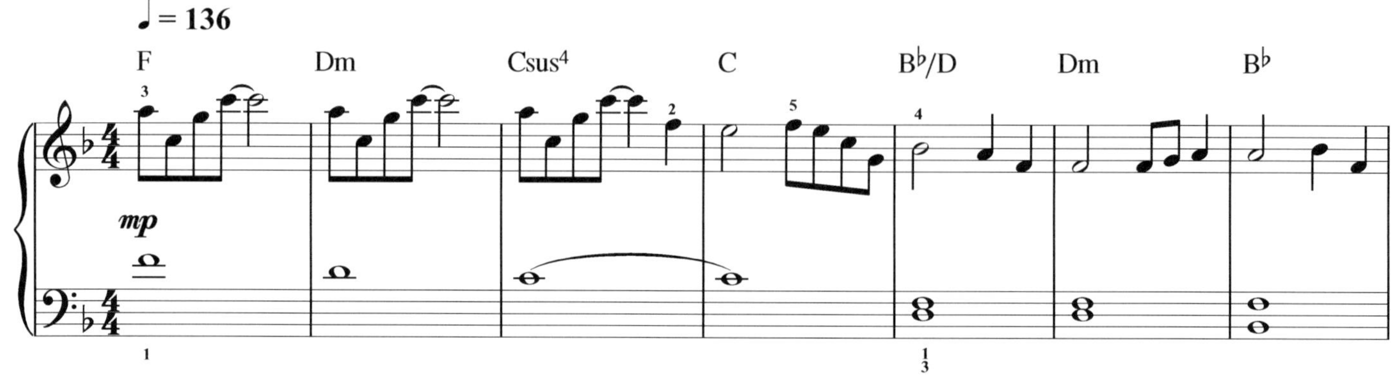

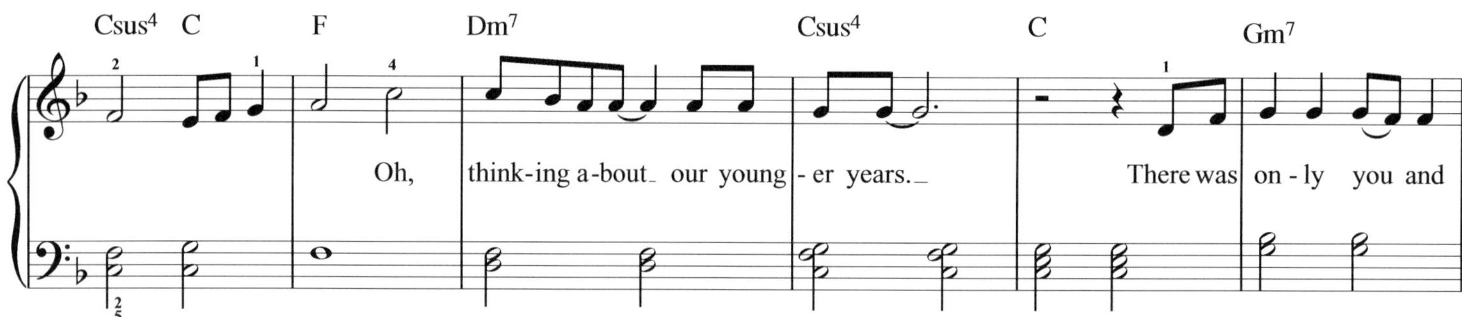

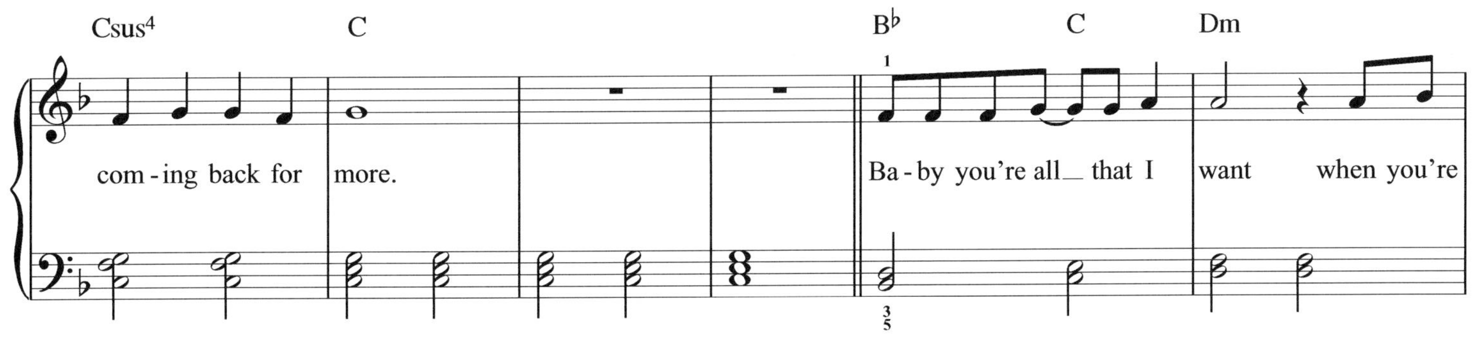

com-ing back for more.
Ba-by you're all__ that I want when you're

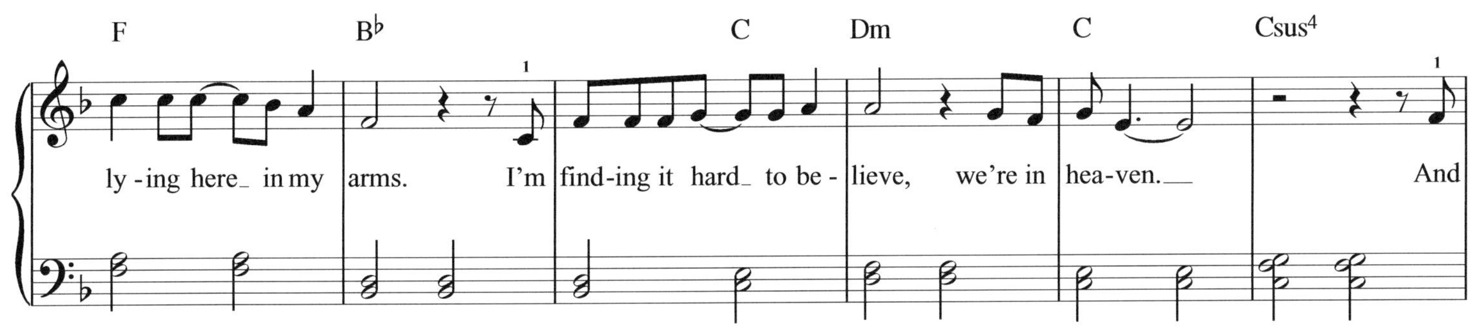

ly -ing here__ in my arms. I'm find-ing it hard__ to be - lieve, we're in hea-ven.__ And

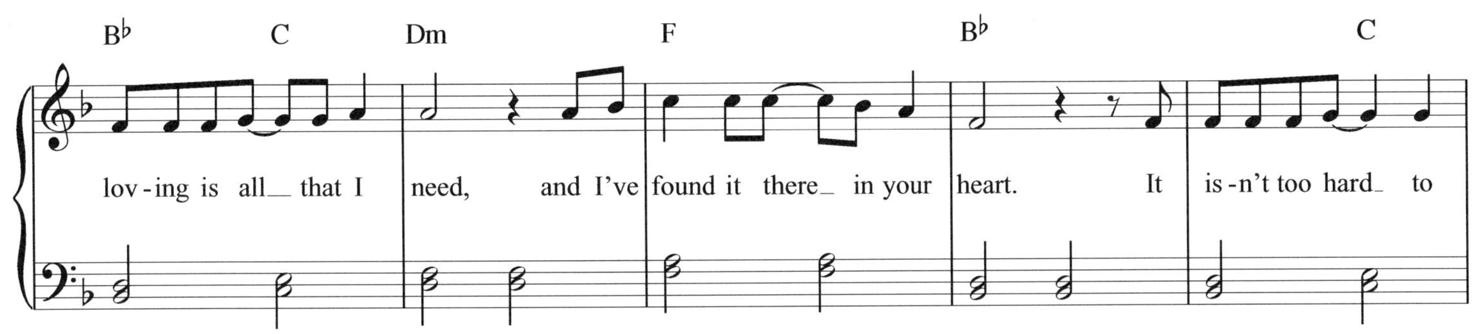

lov-ing is all__ that I need, and I've found it there__ in your heart. It is -n't too hard__ to

see we're in hea-ven.__ Now our dreams are com-ing true, through the

good times and the bad. I'll be stand-ing there by__ you. We're in hea-ven.__

Hey Whatever

Words & Music by Wayne Hector, Steve Mac, Kenneth Papenfus & Carl Papenfus

'Hey Whatever' was recorded by Irish boy-band Westlife in 2003. It reached No.4 and stayed charted for seven weeks.
Westlife formed in 1999 with Nicky Byrne, Shane Filan, Mark Feehily, Kian Egan and now former member
Bryan McFadden. In their search for fame and a record deal the Westlife boys performed in front of Simon Cowell.
Simon was interested in Mark, but didn't think Shane was anything special!

Hints & Tips: This song should be played with a swing feel. Make sure
that left hand notes are not held on into the silent bars.

Am7
D Em7 D/F# G
I pro - fess. But I sing "Hey, what - ev -

D Em7 D/F# G
D Em7 D/F# G N.C.
C G/B Am7 G
- er." Let your beau - ty come a - live, let your col - our fill the sky.

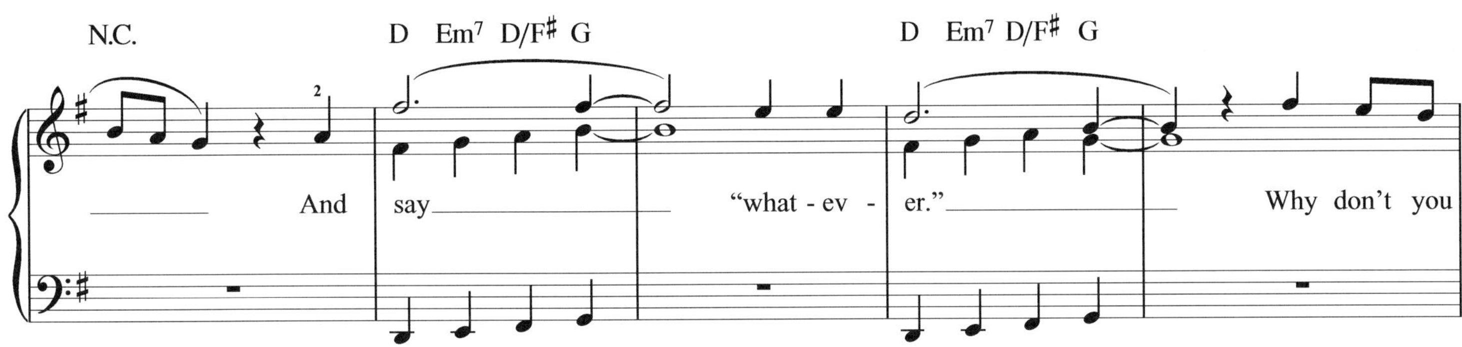

N.C.
D Em7 D/F# G
D Em7 D/F# G
And say "what - ev - er." Why don't you

D Em7 D/F# G N.C.
C G/B Am7 G N.C.
G A
li - ber - ate your mind, let your col - our fill the sky. Ah,

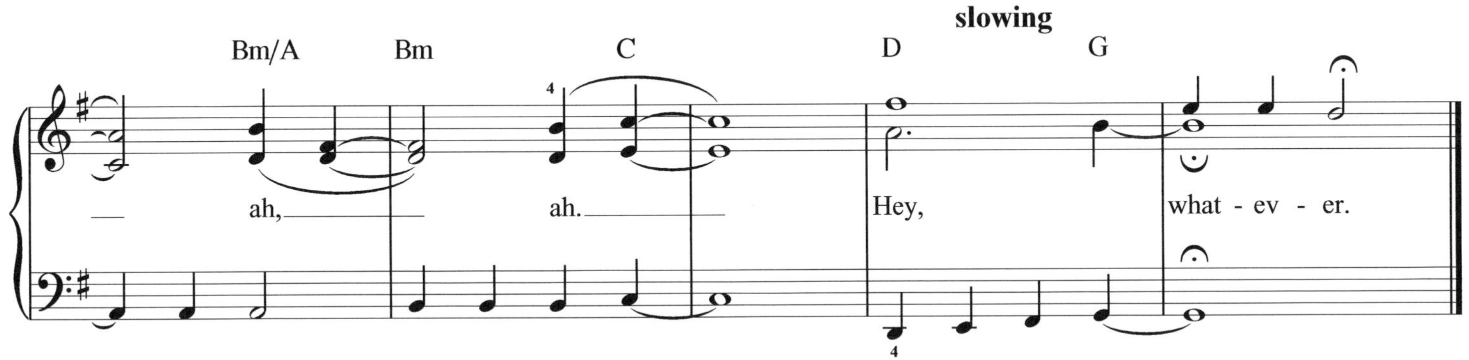

slowing
Bm/A Bm C D G
ah, ah. Hey, what - ev - er.

Hurt

Words & Music by Trent Reznor

'Hurt' was originally recorded by Nine Inch Nails in 1994. This version was recorded by the late country music patriarch Johnny Cash in 2002 for his final album, *The Man Comes Around*. The son of Southern Baptist sharecroppers, Johnny started writing music when he was just 12 years old. He went on to be one of the important figures in country music, creating such classic hits as 'Folsom Prison Blues', 'I Walk The Line', 'A Boy Named Sue' and 'Ring Of Fire'.

Hints & Tips: Try not to make the left hand chords from bar 22 onwards too heavy. The right hand tune must be clearly heard.

F   Gm   Dm   F   Gm   C
kill it all a - way   but I re - mem - ber ev - 'ry - thing.

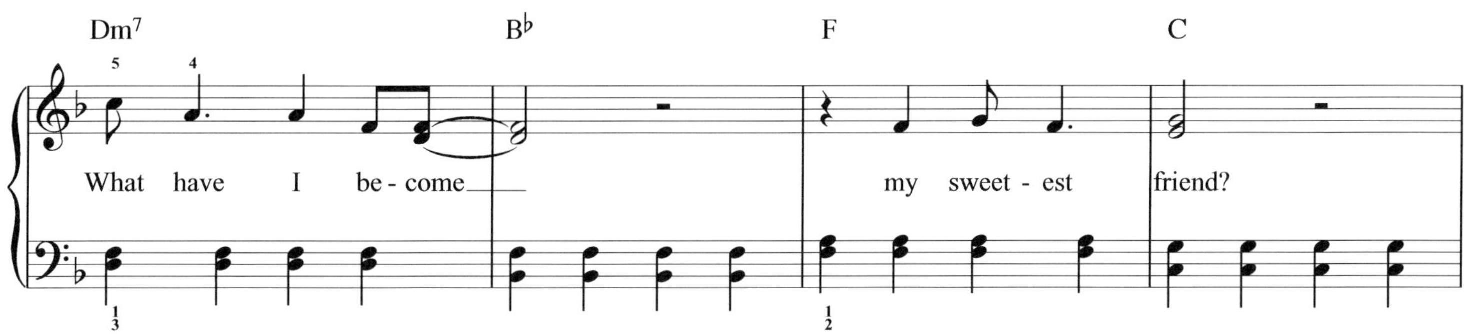

Dm7   B♭   F   C
What have I be - come   my sweet - est friend?

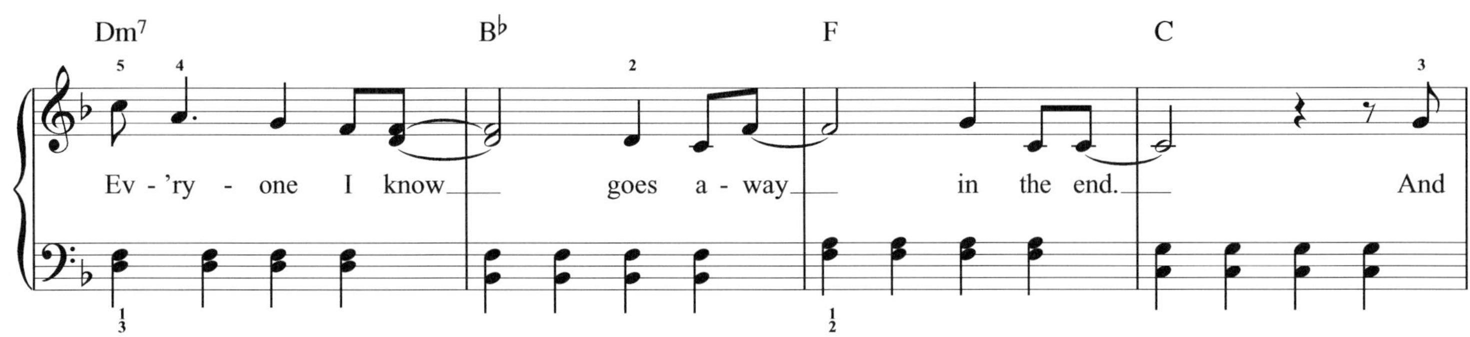

Dm7   B♭   F   C
Ev - 'ry - one I know   goes a - way   in the end.   And

Dm7   B♭   C
you could have it all,   my em - pire of dirt.

Dm7   B♭   C   Dm
I will let you down,   I will make you hurt.

If You're Not The One

Words & Music By Daniel Bedingfield

'If You're Not The One' was recorded by Daniel Bedingfield in 2002 and spent 21 weeks in the charts including one week at No.1. Daniel first graced the UK charts with 'Gotta Get Thru This' in 2001, a song that he created using his own home studio. It stormed in at No.1, remaining in the charts for 18 weeks.
He recently cheated death when his sports car overturned in New Zealand.

Hints & Tips: Sort out the notes in the right hand first of all.
Then practise clapping or tapping the rhythm before putting everything together.

G C
1.
G
through and I hope you are the one I__ share my__ life with.
I don't wan - na run a - way but

Am7 C G Am7 C
I can't take it, I don't un - der - stand. If I'm not made_ for you then why does my heart tell me that I

Em7 D Am7 C
2.
G
am? Is there an - y way_ that I could stay in your arms?__ If And I wish that you could be the_

C G C Dsus C
one I__ die with. And I'm pray - ing you're the one I__ build my_ home with. I hope I love you all my

G Am7 C G Am7
life. I don't wan - na run a - way but I can't take it, I don't un - der - stand. If I'm not made_ for you then

C Em7 D Am7 C
why does my heart tell me that I am? Is there an - y way_ that I could stay in your arms?__

Life For Rent

Words & Music By Dido Armstrong & Rollo Armstrong

'Life For Rent' was recorded and written by Dido Armstrong and her brother Rollo, who is best known for his involvement in the dance act Faithless. Born in London on Christmas Day 1971, Dido has become one of the best-selling solo female artists of all time and her albums, *No Angel* and *Life For Rent*, have so far spent a total of 129 weeks in the charts.

Hints & Tips: If the semiquavers (sixteenth notes) give you trouble, try making up similar patterns using various finger combinations, e.g. 2 & 3, 3 & 4, 4 & 5. Your fingers will soon get stronger.

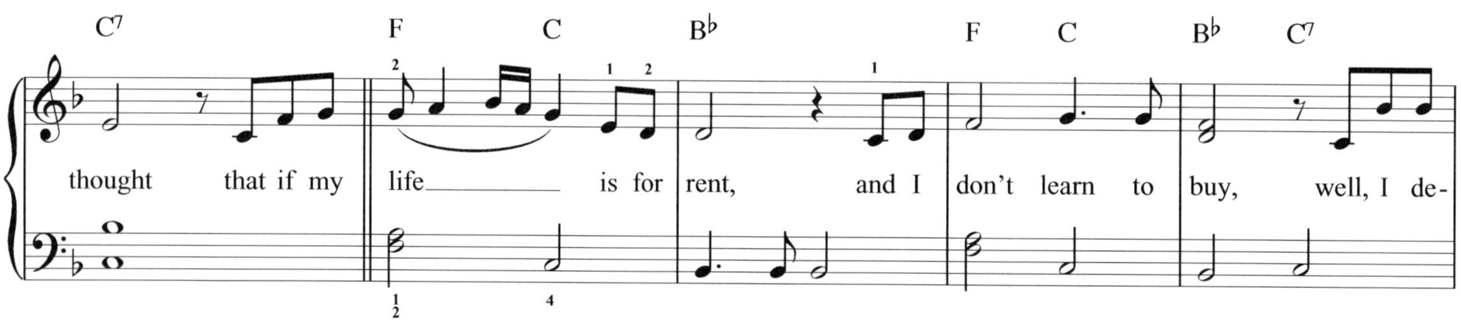

-serve no -thing more than I get 'cause no -thing I have____ is tru -ly mine. I

mine. And if my life____ is__ for rent, and I don't learn to buy,__ well, I de-

- serve no -thing more than I get 'cause no -thing I have____ is tru -ly mine. While my

heart is a shield and I won't let it down while I am so a -fraid to

fail, so I won't ev -en try. Well how can I say I'm a -live.

The Long And Winding Road

Words & Music by John Lennon & Paul McCartney

'The Long And Winding Road' was originally recorded by The Beatles for their final album *Let It Be* and released as a U.S.–only single in 1970. It was No.1 on the Billboard chart for two weeks and spent 10 weeks in the Hot 100. It's been covered by various different artists and this arrangement is based on the version by Pop Idols Will Young & Gareth Gates. It reached No.1 in the charts in October 2002.

Hints & Tips: Keep a very steady tempo (speed) and don't be tempted to rush.
The left hand rhythm in bar two is important and should be brought out.

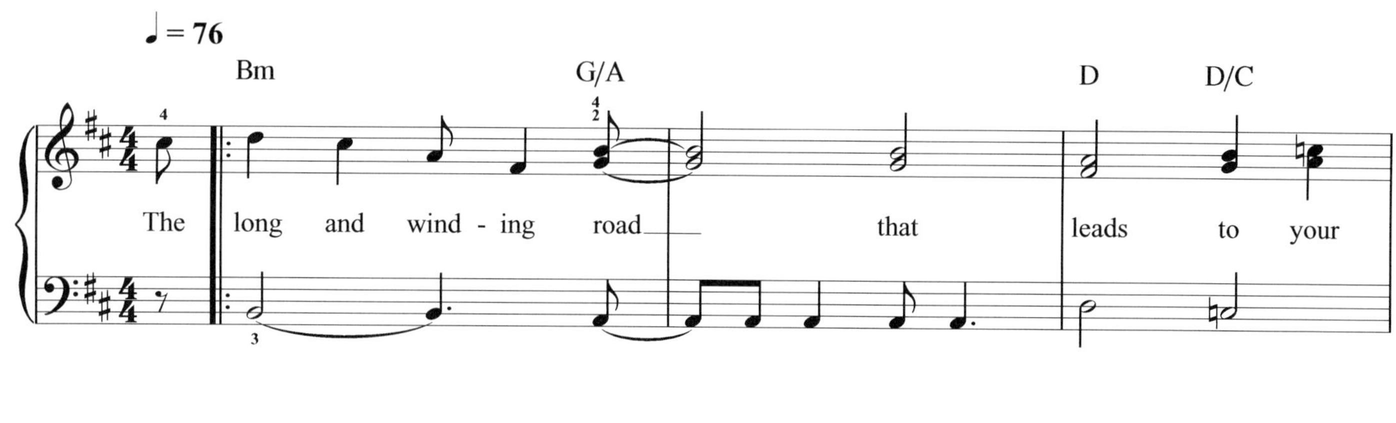

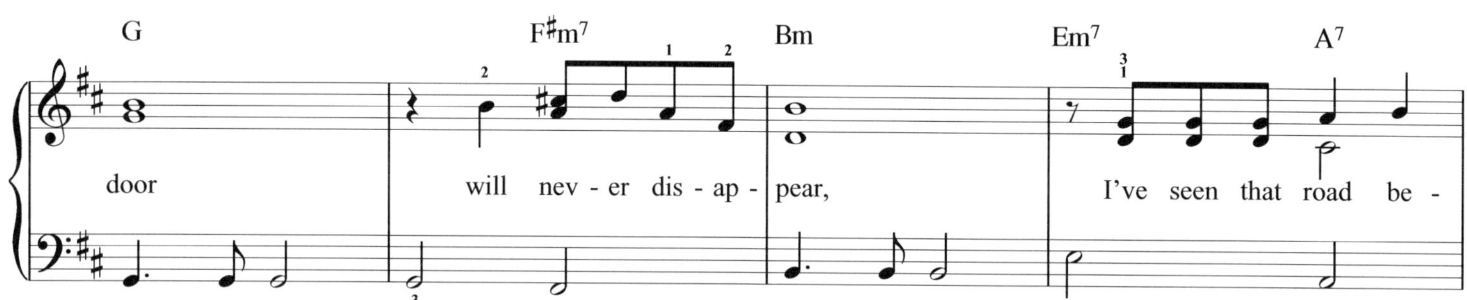

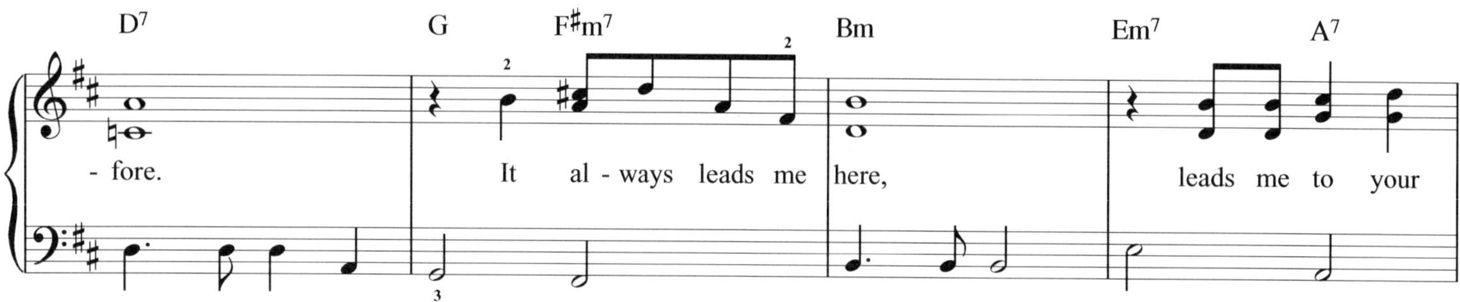

D/A   G   D/F#   Em7 A7   Bm   G/A
An - y - way you'll nev - er know the man - y ways I've tried, but still they lead me back

D   D/C   G   F#m7   Bm
to that long, wind - ing road. you left me stand - ing here

Em7   A7   D7   G   F#m7   Bm
a long long time a - go. Don't leave me wait - ing here,

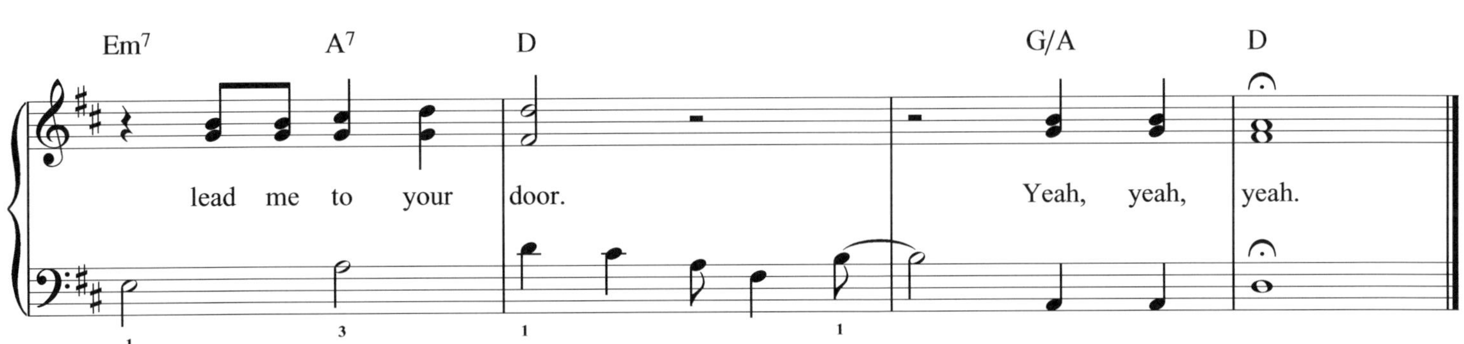

Em7   A7   D   G/A   D
lead me to your door. Yeah, yeah, yeah.

Mad World

Words & Music by Roland Orzabal

'Mad World' was originally recorded by '80s band Tears For Fears in 1982. The arrangement in this book is based on the version by Michael Andrews featuring Gary Jules, which beat The Darkness to become the unexpected Christmas No.1 in 2003. Michael Andrews wrote the music for the 2001 film *Donnie Darko* and brought in old friend Gary Jules to record this song for the soundtrack.

Hints & Tips: The rhythm needs to be really accurate and solid in this song, so that a rather mechanical, almost hypnotic effect is achieved.

Em
G
D
A
Hide my head, I wan-na drown my sor-row, no to-mor-row, no to-mor-row.

Em
A
Em
And I find it kin-da fun-ny, I find it kin-da sad that dreams in which I'm

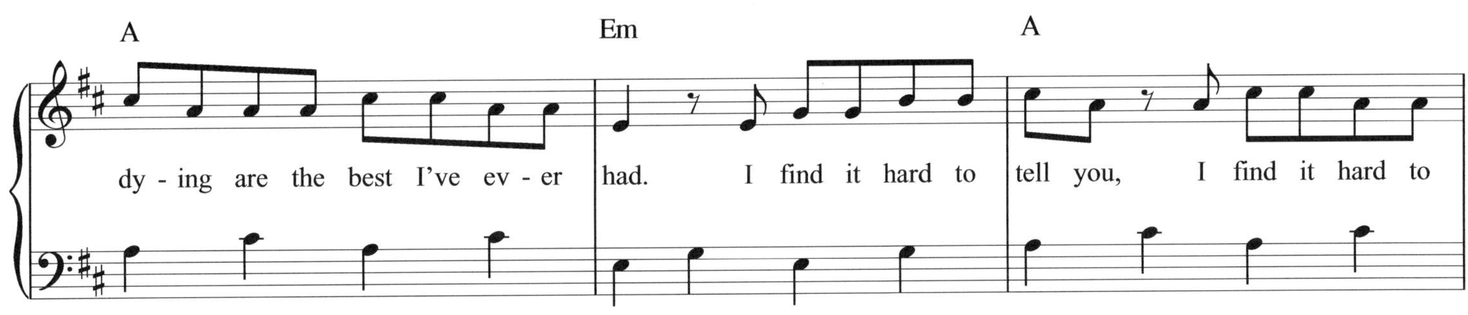

A
Em
A
dy-ing are the best I've ev-er had. I find it hard to tell you, I find it hard to

Em
A
Em
A
take when peo-ple run in cir-cles it's a ve-ry, ve-ry mad world.

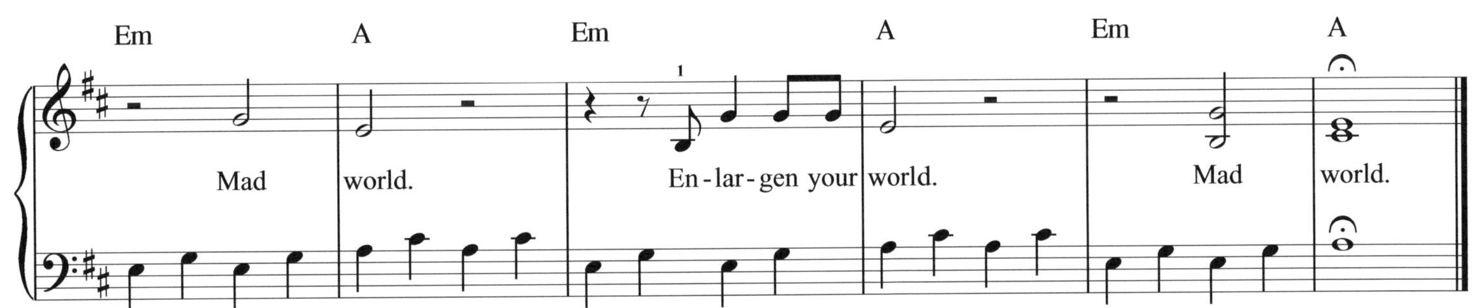

Em
A
Em
A
Em
A
Mad world. En-lar-gen your world. Mad world.

Maybe Tomorrow

Words & Music by Kelly Jones

'Maybe Tomorrow' was a big hit for Welsh band Stereophonics, reaching No.3 in July 2003.
They've released four albums and are famed for being one of the first bands to be signed to Richard Branson's V2 label.
Stereophonics currently consist of just Kelly Jones (vocals, guitars) and Richard Jones (bass).
Former drummer Stuart Cable left the group after their 2003 album, *You Gotta Go There To Come Back*.

Hints & Tips: It is important to feel four beats in a bar in the introduction. If the riff is a problem,
practise it without the tie between the third and fourth notes until you are sure of it.

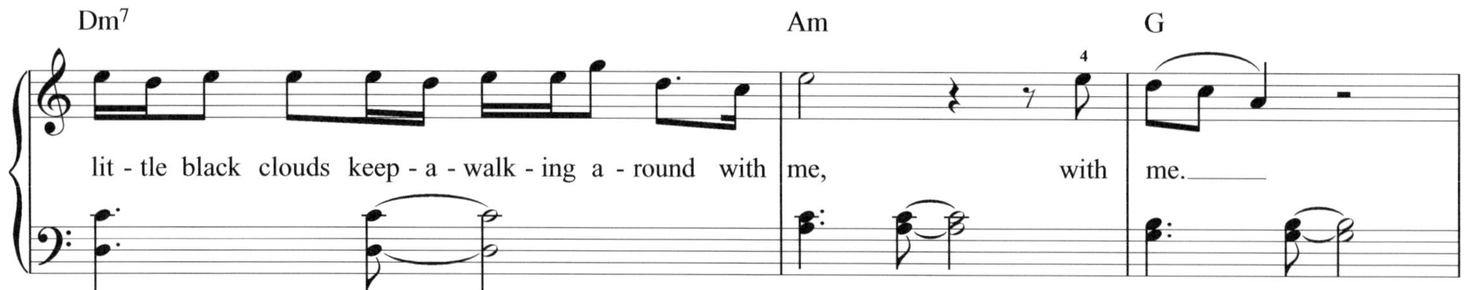

Am
G
F
Dm7
free,   they're all___ free.   So may-be to-mor-row   I'll find my

Am7
G
F
way___________________ home.___   So may-be to-

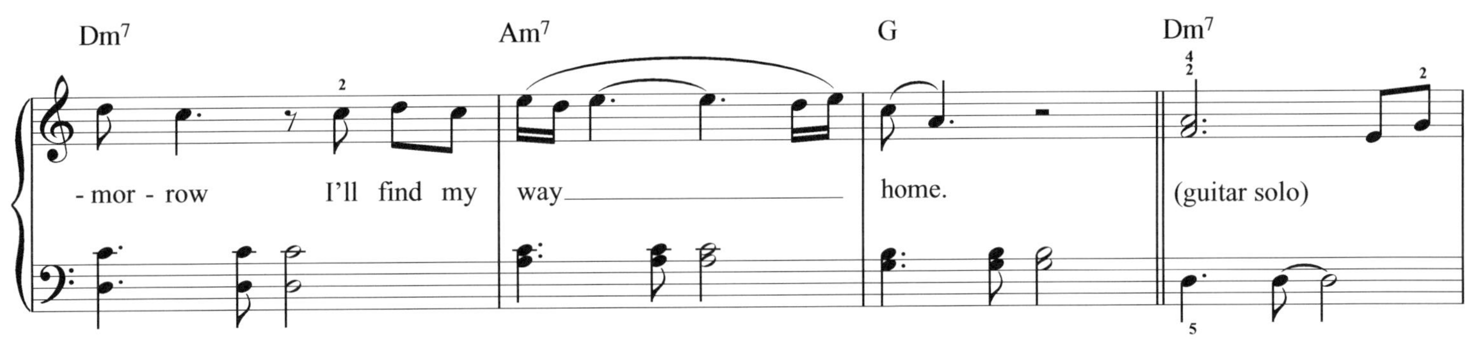

Dm7
Am7
G
Dm7
-mor-row   I'll find my   way___________________ home.   (guitar solo)

E7
Am7
G
Dm7

E7
Am7
Gsus
Fmaj7

Mysterious Girl

Words & Music by Peter Andre, Oliver Jacobs, Phillip Jacobs, Glen Goldsmith & Anthony Wayne

'Mysterious Girl' was first released in 1995 by oily Adonis, Peter Andre. Featuring Bubbler Ranx, the single was only a minor hit until a 1996 re-issue saw it peak at No.2 in the charts. After the success of ITV's *I'm A Celebrity – Get Me Out Of Here!* in 2004 (in which Peter was a contestant), a re-released version of the single made the No.1 spot. Peter was born in England on the February 27, 1973 and then moved to Australia when he was six.

Hints & Tips: A silent third beat is characteristic of this reggae song.
Keep the left hand staccato (short notes) right through.

G   Em⁷   Am⁷   D⁷   G
No doubt you look so fine, oh girl,_ I want to make you mine,_ I want to

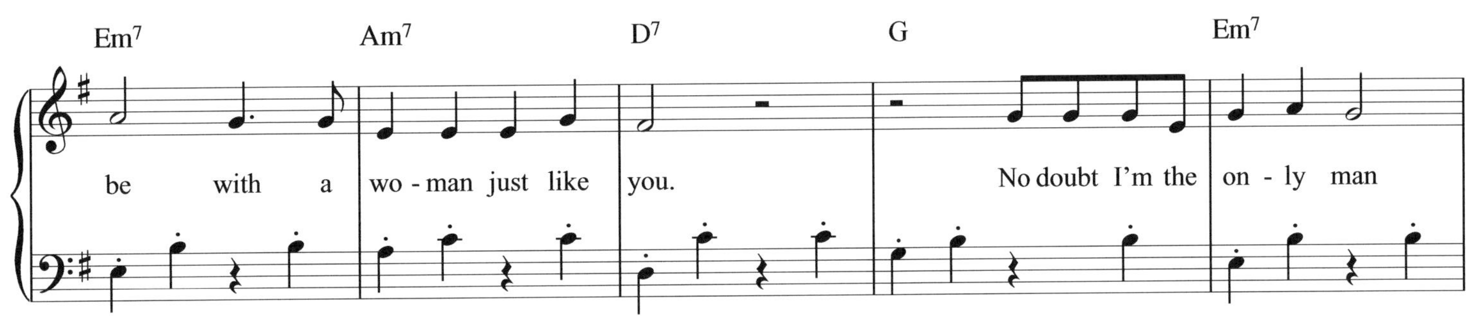

Em⁷   Am⁷   D⁷   G   Em⁷
be with a wo - man just like you. No doubt I'm the on - ly man

Am⁷   D⁷   G   Em⁷   Am⁷
who can love you like I can._ So just let me be with a wo - man that I

D⁷   G   Em⁷   Am⁷   D⁷
love. O,_______ mys - te - ri - ous girl, I wan - na get

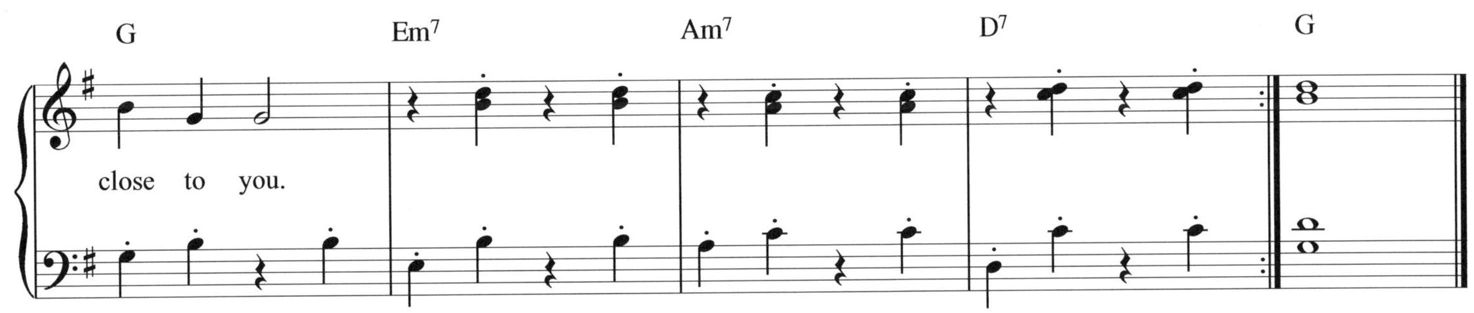

G   Em⁷   Am⁷   D⁷   G
close to you.

She Believes (In Me)

Words & Music by Stephen Gibb

'She Believes In Me' was released by ex-Boyzone member Ronan Keating in 2004. Since leaving Boyzone, Ronan has established himself as a successful television presenter, entrepreneur and solo artist. He is also the co-manager of Irish boy band Westlife. Ronan was born in Dublin on March 3, 1977 and has already written an autobiography, which reached the best-sellers list when he was 23.

Hints & Tips: Take care to hold the right hand semibreves (whole notes) for their full length, until the end of the bar.

Am7   Dm7   G7   C   G7
wakes up to my kiss, and I say it's al-right, and I hold her tight. And she be-
1

C   Bm   E7
-lieves in me, I'll nev-er know just what she sees in me. I told her some-day that she
4   4   5
3

Am   Am/G#   Am/G   Am/F#   F   G7   C
was my girl,_ I could change the world_ with my soul, I was wrong. But she has faith in me,
4
2   3   1   1

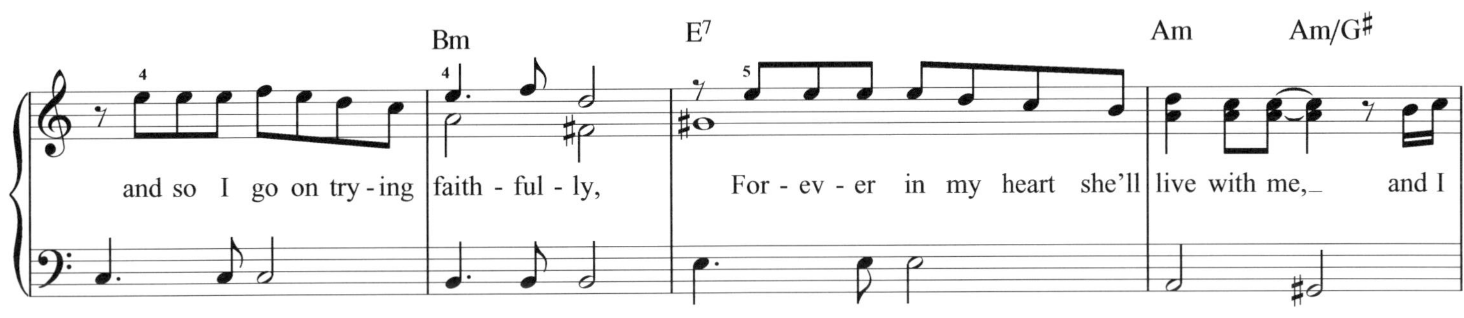

Bm   E7   Am   Am/G#
and so I go on try-ing faith-ful-ly, For-ev-er in my heart she'll live with me,_ and I
4   4   5

Am/G   Am/F#   F   G7   C
hoped and prayed_ I would find a-way,_ find a-way while she lays wait-ing._____
4   5
1   5

Something Beautiful

Words & Music by Robert Williams & Guy Chambers

'Something Beautiful' was a hit for Robbie Williams in 2003 when it reached No.3 in the charts. Robert Peter Williams was born in Stoke-On-Trent on February 13, 1974 and was launched into stardom when he joined Take That, who went on to be one of the most successful bands of the '90s. His solo career, though slow to get off the ground at first, has gone from strength to strength and boasts five No.1 albums and five No.1 singles in the UK.

Hints & Tips: Notice that the tune is played by the left hand until bar 11. Don't play the repeated right hand quaver (eighth note) chords too loudly.

G   G7   C
sign ___ lov - ing kind. ___   Ev - 'ry night you ad - mit
A/C#   G/D   D
de - feat and cry your - self blind. ___   If you
G   G/B   C   D   G
can't wake up in the morn - ing 'cause your bed lies va - cant at night, ___ if you're
D/F# C/E G/D   A/C#   Dsus4 D
lost, hurt, tired or lone - ly, can't con - trol it try as you might. May you
G   B7   Am7   C/G   F
find that love that won't leave ___ you, may you find it by the end of the day, You won't be
G/D D F/C C   Eb   F   G
lost, hurt, tired and lone - ly, some - thing beau - ti - ful will come your ___ way.

Somewhere Only We Know

Words & Music by Tim Rice-Oxley, Tom Chaplin & Richard Hughes

'Somewhere Only We Know' was Keane's first hit single and went in at No.3 in the charts in 2004.
Keane are Tom Chaplin (vocals), Tim Rice-Oxley (piano) and Richard Hughes (drums). All three were at school together
in Hastings and they named the band after a kind old local lady who'd looked after Tom when he was young!

Hints & Tips: Keep the repeated quavers (eighth notes) really steady,
but don't play them too loudly, so that the tune is clearly heard.

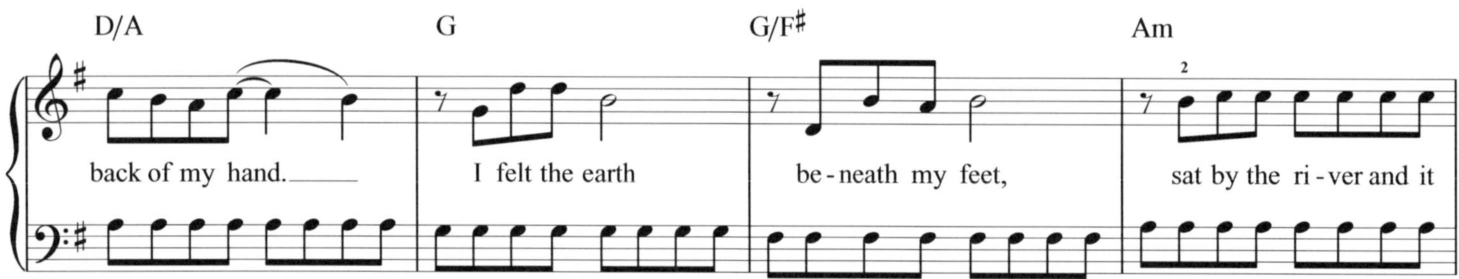

C   D7   Em
I'm get-ting old and I need some-thing to re-ly on.   So tell me when

Bm   C   D7
you're gon-na let me in,   I'm get-ting tired and I need some-where to be-gin.

Am7   G/B   G/D   Am7
And if you have a min-ute why don't we go,   talk a-bout it

G/B   G/D   Am7   G/B   G/D
some-where on-ly we know,   this can't be the end of ev-'ry thing.

C   D   C   G
So why don't we go   some-where on-ly we know.

The Voice Within

Words & Music by Christina Aguilera & Glen Ballard

'The Voice Within' was recorded by dirrty diva Christina Aguilera and reached No.9 in the charts.
It's taken from her highly acclaimed album *Stripped*, which reached No.2 in the UK album charts in 2002.
Christina was born on the December 18, 1980 in Staten Island, New York and, like
Justin and Britney, gained a place as a 'Mouseketeer' on the *Mickey Mouse Club* U.S. TV show, aged 12.

Hints & Tips: Make sure that the notes in the left hand chords sound exactly together.
Hold the right hand minims (half notes) their full value.

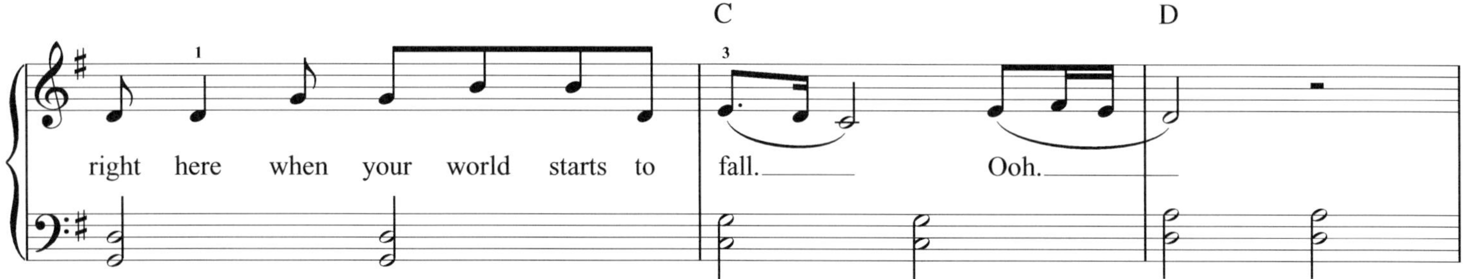

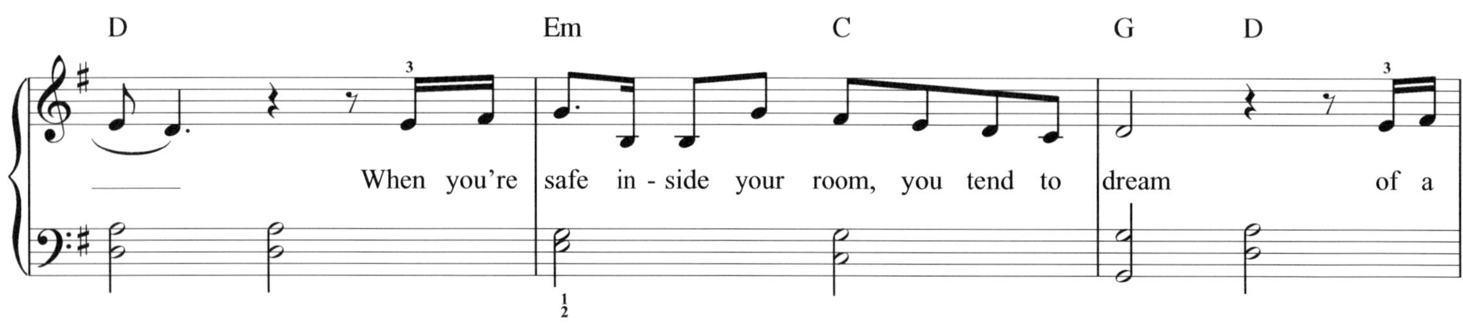

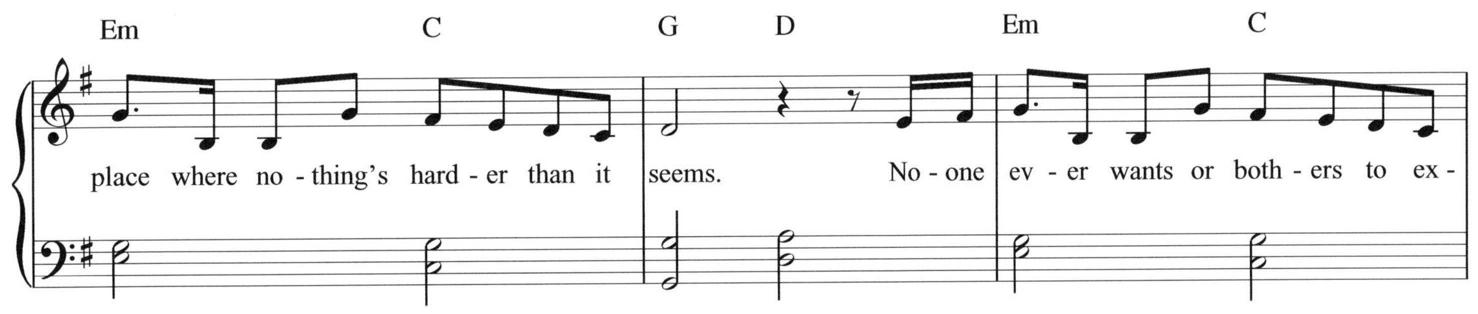

Em   C   G   D   Em   C
place where no - thing's hard - er than it seems.   No - one ev - er wants or both - ers to ex -

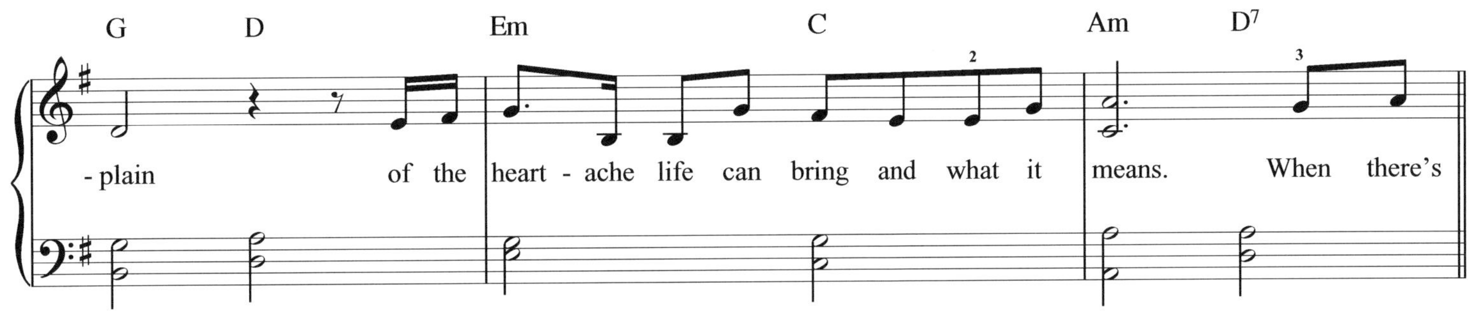

G   D   Em   C   Am   D7
- plain   of the heart - ache life can bring and what it means.   When there's

G   Cm   Em   G7   A7
no - one else, look in - side your - self;   like your old - est friend,_ just

Cm   D7   G   Cm   Em   G7
trust the voice with - in. Then you'll find the strength that will guide your way   if

A7   Cm   D7   G
you'll learn to be - gin____ to   trust the voice with - in.

With A Little Help From My Friends

Words & Music by John Lennon & Paul McCartney

'With A Little Help From My Friends' was originally recorded by The Beatles on March 29, 1967.
The second track on the classic *Sgt. Pepper's Lonely Hearts Club Band* album, it was sung by Ringo Starr
under the moniker of Billy Shears. Although The Beatles did not release it as a single, it has proved to
be one of their most enduring and successful songs; cover versions by Joe Cocker, Wet Wet Wet and Pop Idol
runners-up Sam & Mark have all reached No.1 as a single (in 1968, 1988 and 2004 respectively).

Hints & Tips: Keep relaxed and play this old Beatles song with a gentle swing feel.

C   Am   D7   C   B♭   F   N.C.
friends. Do you need an - y - bod - y? I need some - bod - y to love. Could it

Am   D7   C   B♭   F
be an - y - bod - y? I want some - bod - y to love.

C   G   Dm   G7
Would you be - lieve_ in a love at first sight? Yes, I'm cer - tain that it hap - pens all the

C   G   Dm   G7
time. What do you see_ when you turn out the light?_ I can't tell you but I know it's

C   B♭/F   F   C
mine. Oh I get by with a lit - tle help from my friends. I get

B♭/F   F   C   F   C
high with a lit - tle help from my friends. I'm gon - na try with a lit - tle help from my friends.

Cry Me A River

Words & Music By Justin Timberlake, Scott Storch & Tim Mosley

'Cry Me A River' was recorded by Justin Timberlake and charted at No.2 in February 2003, remaining in the charts for a further 12 weeks. Justin was born on January 31, 1981 in Memphis, Tennessee and started his show-biz career as a 'Mousekateer' on the *Mickey Mouse Club* - a U.S. children's show. He was catapulted into the dizzy heights of fame when he joined teeny-pop boy band *NSYNC, which paved the way towards his hugely successful solo career as we know it.

Hints & Tips: Some of the rhythms are pretty tricky here, so practise the right hand on its own. It may help you if you mark the beats by tapping with your left hand or foot.

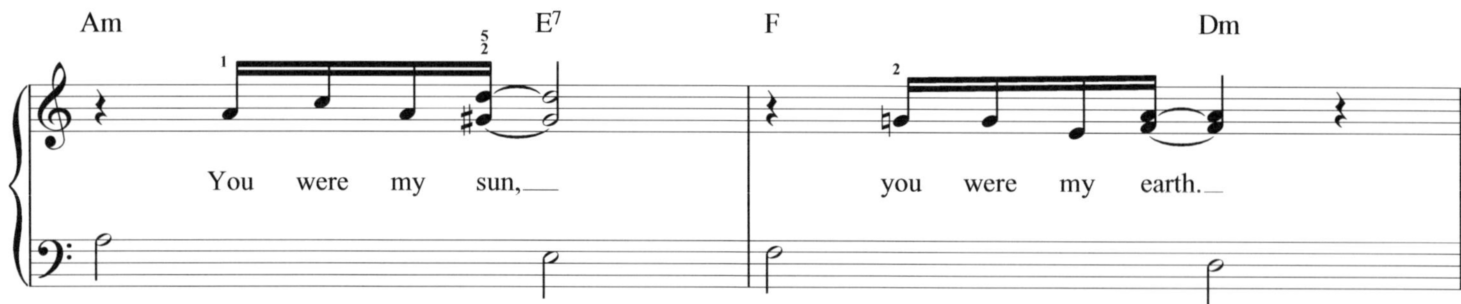

F
Dm
Am
E7
and made oth - er plans.___
But I bet you did - n't think   that they would come crash -

F
Dm
Am
E7
- ing down, no.
You don't have to say   what you did.   I

F
Dm
Am
E7
al - rea - dy know   I found out from him.
Now there's just no chance   for you and me,   there'll

F
Dm
Am
Dm
nev - er be   and don't it make you sad a - bout it? Told me you love_ me, why did you leave_

F
G
Am
Dm
F
G
___ me all a - lone?
Now you tell me you need_ me when you call me on the phone.

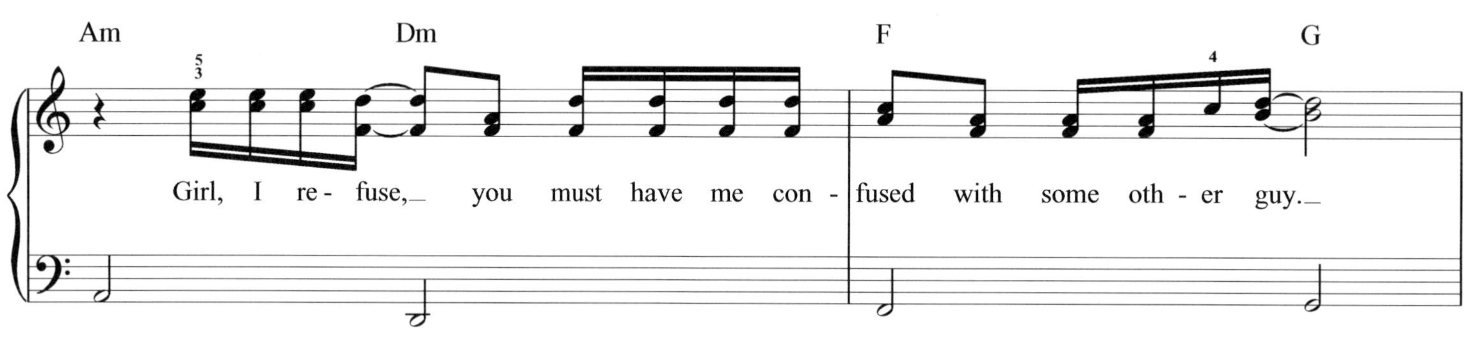

Am   Dm   F   G
Girl, I re - fuse,_ you must have me con - fused with some oth - er guy._

Am   Dm   F   G
Your brid - ges were burned,_ now it's your turn___ to cry. Cry me a riv -

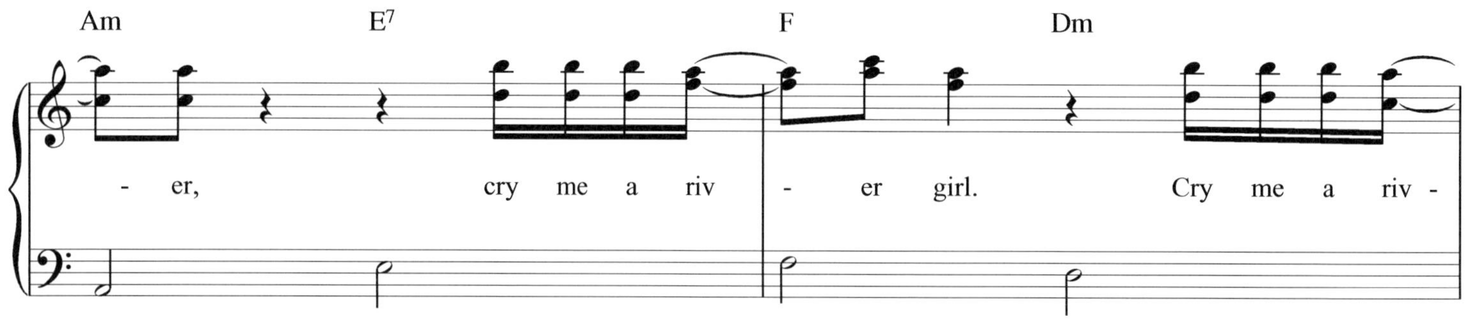

Am   E7   F   Dm
- er,   cry me a riv - er girl.   Cry me a riv -

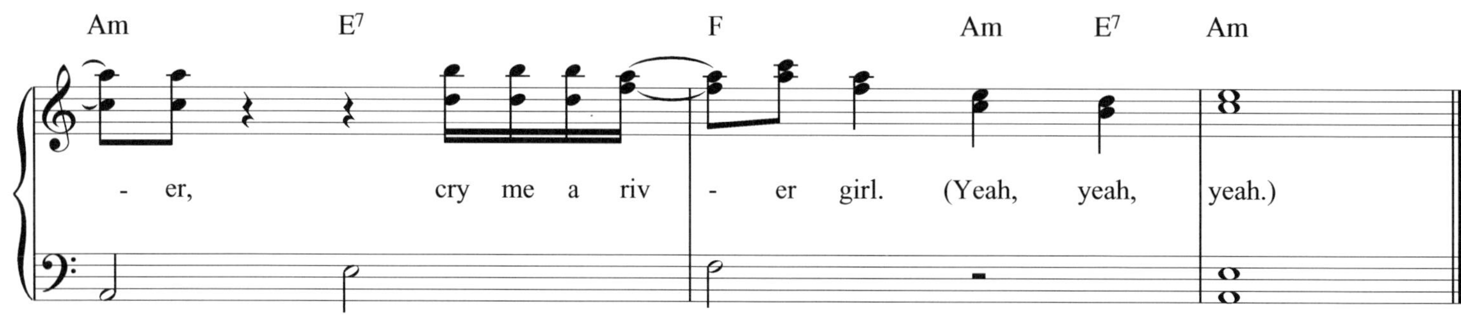

Am   E7   F   Am   E7   Am
- er,   cry me a riv - er girl. (Yeah, yeah, yeah.)